THE STRATEGY, IMPACT & MINISTRY OF LOCAL CHRISTIAN RADIO

POWERFUL CHRISTIAN RADIO

Josh Reid

The Strategy, Impact & Ministry of Local Christian Radio

Foreword by Phil Cooke

POWERFUL CHRISTIAN RADIO

POWERFUL CHRISTIAN RADIO

The Strategy, Impact & Ministry
of Local Christian Radio

Josh Reid

Foreword by Phil Cooke

POWERFUL CHRISTIAN RADIO

PRAISE FOR **POWERFUL CHRISTIAN RADIO**

Josh Reid has "cracked the code" on the purpose, function and power of Christian Radio to influence and positively impact culture. When you understand WHY Christian Radio exists, it brings greater clarity to HOW it goes about doing WHAT it does.

Brett McLeod, CEO, 96five Family Radio

This book covers a topic you won't currently find on bookshelves, but is well communicated and a very easy read.

Kim Wilkinson, Marketing Manager, Hope Media

Love this book. Very comprehensive and shows the potential of Christian Radio. Excellent.

Peter Pilt, Senior Pastor, Nowra City Church

I love this book. It spells out well how Christian Radio works & really needs to be available for all Christians so they can get an understanding of Christian media.

Darren Robinson, Veteran Radio Broadcaster, Pulse 94.1

Josh has managed to encapsulate some of the stories and impact of how powerful the radio waves can be and will continue to be in the future.

Brett Ryan, CEO, Focus on the Family - Australia

Copyright

© 2014 by Joshua Samuel Reid

All rights reserved. No portion of this book may be reproduced, stored in a retrieval system, or transmitted in any form or by any means – electronic, mechanical, photocopy, recording, scanning, or other – except for brief quotations in critical reviews or articles, without the prior written permission of the publisher.

Disclaimer: The opinions presented in this book are the sole opinions of the author and may not necessarily reflect the position of your local Christian Radio station, nor the organizations the author may work for or with at various times.

Published in Wollongong, Australia, by Josh Reid Media. Josh Reid Media is a registered trademark of Earl Street Pictures Pty Ltd.

Josh Reid Media titles may be purchased in bulk for educational, business, fund-raising, or sales promotional use. For information, please email josh@joshreidmedia.com.

National Library of Australia Cataloguing-in-Publication entry:

Author: Reid, Josh, 1974- author.

Title: Powerful Christian Radio : the strategy, impact & ministry of local Christian radio / Josh Reid ;
foreword by Phil Cooke.
ISBN-13: 978-0992469214 (paperback)
ISBN-10:   099246921X

Notes: Includes bibliographical references and index.
Subjects: Religious broadcasting--Christianity.
Religious broadcasting--Australia.
Radio in religion--Australia.
Radio stations—Australia.
Other Authors/Contributors:
Cooke, Phil, 1954- writer of introduction.
Dewey Number: 791.45682

Dedicated to Michael Randall

POWERFUL CHRISTIAN RADIO

Table of Contents

Praise For Powerful Christian Radio........................1

Foreword by Phil Cooke: Radio Matters for the Future of the Church..11

PART ONE: Understanding Christian Radio...........15
   1. Is Christian Radio really a Ministry?...............17
   2. How does Media Influence Us?.......................23
   3. The Strategy of Christian Radio.....................35
   4. Real Stories: Lives Changed through Christian Radio..41

PART TWO: Using Christian Radio..........................51
   5. The 21st Century Church................................53
   6. Christian Radio in Friendship Evangelism.....61
   7. 11 Ways the Church can Partner with Christian Radio..69
   8. Importance of Supporting Christian Radio.....93

Credits...100
Acknowledgments..101
About the Author..104

POWERFUL CHRISTIAN RADIO

Foreword by Phil Cooke

Radio Matters for the Future of the Church

In a world that's gone Internet crazy it's easy to convince churches and ministries about the importance of using web strategies or social media as evangelism tools. After all, with more than one billion users, Facebook is now the third largest country in the world, which means it's time to start sending missionaries and planting churches in that country. Online evangelism is an easy sell to a new generation of pastors and leaders who have been posting their lives online since childhood.

But lost in the Internet frenzy is the power of *traditional* media – particularly radio. We've certainly moved from the era of 'mass media' to the era of 'customized media.' People want to program their own song lists, podcasts, and online content. Fine. I get that. But it's interesting that human beings are still random creatures and absolutely love surprises.

In my car for instance, I have Bluetooth, plus every connector imaginable. I can listen to CDs, DVDs, iPods, iPhones – whatever. However as tech savvy as I am, the thing I listen to 95% of the time? Old fashioned radio.

I'm not sure if I can explain it, but the truth is, I like the surprise of not knowing what's coming up next. And when it comes to *Christian Radio*, I love the teaching, the community news and updates on what God is doing in my city.

The bottom line is that we're finding that in a digital age, traditional media like radio and TV are the last great camp-fires of our culture. When people are on the web, they're looking at literally billions of *different* websites. But when it comes to traditional media, there's a limited number of radio and TV channels, so trust me – those channels are delivering large audiences. It's one reason that major sporting events, special event programming like the Oscars, or concerts still draw huge ratings.

Which leads me to Josh Reid's book **"Powerful Christian Radio."** This isn't just Josh's take on media, it's required reading if your goal is to impact this culture with a message of hope. The Internet may be getting all the publicity these days, but radio is alive and well. Plus, with digital delivery, radio programming is being heard in more and more places around the world.

Do yourself a favor and read this book. Josh has a long track record exploring how media connects with people, so I'm interested in what he has to say. And when it comes to engaging your community or audience with the gospel, radio is easy to produce, inexpensive to buy time, and reaches people in unexpected moments – like in the car, or in the background at work.

I've written before that in the evolution of media, movies didn't replace live events, radio didn't replace movies, TV didn't replace radio, and online delivery won't replace TV. Every media platform finds its own level and reaches its own audience.

That's why radio may be the most potent platform for your message. In the pages that follow, you'll discover information you didn't know, and see the potential of a channel that you've probably forgotten.

Either way, this is your second chance. Take it.

Phil Cooke

Filmmaker, media consultant, and author of *"Unique: Telling Your Story in the Age of Brands and Social Media."*
www.philcooke.com

PART ONE
Understanding Christian Radio

POWERFUL CHRISTIAN RADIO

Chapter 1

Is Christian Radio *really* a Ministry?

I'll be the first to admit that most church pastors, as well as a lot of church attending Christians, don't see the local Christian Radio station as a ministry. How *do* they see it? They see that it's a nice thing to have. For instance, people might say, "Oh isn't it great that we have a Christian Radio station that we can tune in to and hear nice music", or, "It's safe for my kids to listen to, it's family friendly, that's what it's all about." Now, both those thoughts are perfectly valid, but they're **not** what Christian Radio is *really* all about.

So... what is it about?

At its core it is a strategic, very powerful, influential ministry, that through media broadcast, communicates with thousands of people every day, reaching into places where the local church can never go.

It is **the Media Arm** of the local church.

What will I hear on Christian Radio?

Now people may have all sorts of notions about what 'Christian Radio' sounds like. There *are* a few different styles, but today you would rarely find one that only plays old hymns or preaching all day long. Today's Christian Radio plays a contemporary mix of current popular songs, making it very attractive to a wider audience. Some stations play 100% Christian record labels (that is – what we call *Christian music*) having a ministry of encouraging Christians. Other stations will play around 40% Christian labels and then 60% mainstream artists (*secular music*). The latter tending to be evangelism focused – attracting non-churched listeners with music they already know.

But no matter what style *your* local Christian Radio station chooses to be, it is still an important ministry, and this book sets out to explain *how* that ministry really works.

Why is Christian Radio so important for the local church? Or for that matter, to us as individual Christian believers?

Because it works *alongside* the local church, in strategic pre-evangelism. Because it attracts people who don't normally attend *any* church. Because it reaches people in places that the local church can never go. Because it has a subtle evangelistic ministry, which means most people are open to listening, even if they are closed about attending church. Because it *prepares* people to receive the gospel message *before* they are ready to hear it.

While there are times that God uses Christian Radio to bring someone to faith, it is not the primary purpose. Christian Radio is designed to be subtly evangelistic through entertainment. It gently prepares the hearts and minds of listeners to receive the gospel, and local churches bring the one-to-one discipleship and Biblical teaching needed to achieve spiritual maturity – what a powerful combination!

If you or I asked some of our family and friends to church, they might say, "...what are you talking about?... no way... if I step into a church the roof will cave in." We've all heard many excuses. But... through listening to Christian Radio their minds will get full of good, uplifting, Bible based songs and content - and over time **they become open to the Gospel message**; to Christianity and to God.

Christian Radio *is* an influential ministry which communicates through media broadcast, presenting itself as entertainment.

Christian Radio is...

- A powerful far reaching ministry.
- The media arm of the local church.
- Going into places the local church can never go.
- Working alongside the church in pre-evangelism.
- A contemporary mix of popular music.
- Attractive to non-church attending listeners.
- Used to *prepare* people to *receive* the gospel.

POWERFUL CHRISTIAN RADIO

Chapter 2

How does Media Influence Us?

From Hollywood films and TV shows, to magazines and music, - modern media has been influencing us for a very long time. This is not a *bad* thing as such – but what I'm emphasizing in this chapter is **the need for *us* to understand** the power that it *does* have.

Any Hollywood studio executive, anybody leading a large media organization, any radio program director, recognizes that media is all about *influence*. Even though it looks like (or sounds like) entertainment, it's really all about **influencing culture**.

Why does advertising at the Super Bowl cost millions of dollars? Because it works! It gets though to people. **Media influences culture - and it does so very subtly, yet effectively**. Media will not often tell you directly what to wear or think or say or do. But it will tell you a story which presents you with a thought, an idea. These stories are designed to trigger something in your mind which sets you on a path towards changing your thinking and activity. Consumers of media are influenced by the messages in these stories because they are presented as entertainment, not philosophy.

The subtle messages presented through media can change the worldview of individuals, and over a generation, culture and law.

The number 1 rule with media is that it's about influence - not really about entertainment. However, **it still has to *be* entertainment**. It is influence through entertainment. Influence through media. Look at your 'national news' service or all those 'current affairs' shows. Yes they cover important issues, but they have a HUGE entertainment value to them.

In Robert McKee's book *Story: Substance, structure, style, and the principles of screenwriting*, he explains how Plato, the famous Greek philosopher, argued that all poets and storytellers should be expelled from the city; he wanted them gone! (Which is a little ironic, as he told some pretty good stories himself.)

Plato argued that a philosopher in his time, would stand up on his soapbox in the city square, and proclaim, in great detail, exactly what he believed. Clearly outlining his beliefs so that there was nothing hidden in his message. This is a little like preaching a sermon today – we outline our points clearly, and carefully check our references, checking its accuracy, so that every sentence can be easily explained, understood and stand up to criticism.

But Plato argued that poets and storytellers also have a message, - one which is hidden. He claimed that although they appear to simply be entertainment, they are **really about influence**. A nice little fairytale still has a moral to it, and therefore it still influences. Instead of the message being clear and direct like a *proper* philosopher, their messages are hidden, woven into the fabric of the story.

And so even though their message is hidden and only comes through subtly, **the message still influences**. And people begin to change their minds because of the hidden message in the story. And what's worse, Plato claimed, is that because their messages are hidden and not out in the open like a philosopher, the message is received at a deeper, sub-conscious level, and so changes people's core beliefs and values.

We don't have philosophers standing up in the middle of the mall these days. And church attendance is way down, decreasing each year. So our teacher's and pastor's circle of influence is getting smaller and smaller. **Today our biggest and most effective influencers are modern media.** The storytellers of today are Hollywood films, TV shows and music; they are the ones who influence us at our deepest level. They are the ones who change people's core beliefs.

The power of media's influence on our thinking and culture has been observed for many years.

In the book *Jolt: Get the jump on a world that's constantly changing,* Phil Cooke highlights Robert Johnston's observations:

> As early as 1934, in the movie *It Happened One Night*, popular star Clark Gable acted in the movie without an undershirt to better display his physique and, thereafter, undershirt sales dropped dramatically nationwide. In fact, it was not until World War II when the military retrained men to wear undershirts that the crippled industry finally recovered.
>
> And in 1942, when Walt Disney's animated feature *Bambi* premiered, deer hunting in America dropped from a $5.7 million business to barely $1 million. (What kid would let his dad shoot Bambi?)

So the influence that media has on our culture is nothing new. And as people who are concerned about what's influencing us, we need to understand how it works. We need to be aware of the hidden messages that are coming through our modern media. And we need to learn how to put *our* message into media effectively.

How do messages get 'hidden' in media these days?

The best example to use is a movie script (a screenplay) because every professional screenwriter uses something McKee calls, the *Controlling Idea*. I suppose this is another way to say 'theme' or 'message', but I like that phrase better as it really describes exactly what happens **when you put a *thought* into a film**. The *Controlling Idea* is what a screenwriter has before a word hits the page.

It is what they have before developing any characters, structuring the screenplay, or writing any dialogue. They have this even before they decide what genre the film will be. It is the idea or philosophy which the whole film is centered around.

It is like an argument or point of view put forward, which the film provides an answer for. I like the term *Controlling Idea* because it really does determine what idea the audience leaves with.

How do these 'hidden messages' affect us when we view or listen to media?

It's what we walk away with. Not necessarily a conscious thought or verbal expression, but more like the whole feeling that you get when you leave the cinema. (Or finish listening to a song.) **It leaves a thought with you that you keep thinking about.**

For example, you may go and see a movie which leads you to thinking about something in your own life.

> "Oh, wasn't that great when the hero saved the village, wouldn't it be great if I could do something like that locally?"

> "How that guy built his house in the film is a bit like how I'm trying to build my business."

"When that alien sacrificed himself to save the planet of fuzzy creatures, is like how I need to put my family's interests ahead of my own."

"That children's cartoon reminded me to be a better dad."

"I do need to treat my wife more like that cat owner treated her cat." (Take that how you want it!)

So people will walk out of a cinema either thinking to themselves, "I'd like to be a bit more like that", or, "Wouldn't it be great if somebody in the community did that?", or, "Wouldn't it be great if our mayor was like that film mayor", or, "Maybe it would be better if we didn't have a government", and the list goes on.

Media is not just entertainment – it leaves us with an idea that we take away with us, at a very deep level.

How does media affect Christians and Christian culture?

Christians are generally portrayed in the media as irrelevant or ridiculous. A good example is the comedy film *Four Weddings and a Funeral*. This is a very funny film which perhaps makes the message received even more powerful – because with comedy we *really do* think it's simply entertainment - and we're certainly not expecting it to change our thinking.

In the film there are two characters who represent the church, and therefore they represent Jesus Christ. Both of these characters are Church of England ministers. The first one, a novice priest, is played by Rowan Atkinson (a.k.a. Mr. Bean) and he just gets everything wrong and looks ridiculous. And it's funny, it's hilarious. **But this is what it is really doing** – portraying church ministers as ridiculous. It suggests to the viewer that God's church on earth (and therefore what Christians believe about God) is ridiculous.

People will watch this film and think, "Oh, the church *is* crazy isn't it?", or, "Hey, I know some crazy old preachers like that."

Towards the end of the film we see another Church of England minister. This time we see a serious and boring minister leading a funeral. He mutters something irrelevant, and then sits down. Then a friend of the deceased (who happens to be homosexual) stands up and gives the most powerful, emotional, tear-jerking speech of the whole film. This is what is happening here – **the film portrays the church leader (and therefore the church and God) as boring and irrelevant, and providing no real answers**. Then, it strongly suggests that the answers we seek can be found elsewhere.

This is where the *Controlling Idea* comes in. The church, the minister, Christianity and God, are ridiculous and have nothing relevant to say to our modern culture.

As Christians we cannot afford to be naive about the messages hidden inside media. We can't just assume that we are, *'just seeing the messages that we want to see'*, but other people see different messages. The message is already there – hidden, woven into the fabric of the film, or song, reaching out to influence you and the rest of our culture, with their particular beliefs.

Media influences our culture by placing hidden messages inside entertaining stories, - and this strategy influences us and our culture at a deep sub-conscious level.

Media Influences Culture by...

- Presenting itself as entertainment.
- Placing *Hidden Thoughts* inside entertainment.
- Subtly suggesting what we should think and do.
- Communicating to thousands or millions of people.
- Being the philosophers of our time.

POWERFUL CHRISTIAN RADIO

Chapter 3

The Strategy of Christian Radio

So by now we understand that Christian Radio *is* a ministry, and we understand the powerful influence that media has on our culture. Knowing these two factors, how does Christian Radio *choose* to minister *through* media?

As Christians we can sometimes forget that not everyone grows up in a churched culture. In fact most people don't. We no longer live in a 'Christian society', and people today do not even know the basics of the Christian story.

What this means is that people don't know who the latest Christian pop-stars are, they don't know praise and worship songs, they have never heard of all your favorite preachers. They aren't driving around with Christian teaching CDs or music in their car. And they aren't attending church at all. How then do we reach them?

This is where Christian Radio comes in. **We are like media missionaries.** Instead of being sent to some foreign land to minister to the pagans, we are sent via radio waves and Internet streaming to the un-churched people in our own city. As like the missionaries of old, we also go to a people and culture who are foreign to the Christian message. Going into places that the local church can not reach by themselves.

Picture this - somebody is alone, driving in their car, they switch on the radio and tune in to any station they wish. No one is watching them. No matter what reputation they might have with their family or friends, no matter what prejudices they might have, no matter what their values and beliefs are, **they can simply switch on the radio, scan through the channels, and stumble across the local Christian Radio station.**

And do you know what the *safe* thing is for them?

Nobody will ever know they are listening to Christian Radio. It can't be traced, it's not being recorded, there will be no evidence left. They are safe to choose to listen to it as they please.

The local church is like God's infantry in a battle, working on the front lines, battling and striving against the enemy to get the gospel through to people who need freedom. **But any good army knows they also need the Air Force.** Christian Radio is God's Air Force, providing air cover for the infantry, clearing the way ahead of the troops to make the battle easier to fight and enabling victory. (Christian Radio literally broadcasting across the air.)

I also like to use a farming metaphor **to illustrate the strategy of Christian Radio** - understanding where it fits into God's overall plan. In church circles we are familiar with terms like planting the seed, reaping the harvest etc. **Christian Radio works *before* the seed is planted.** We prepare the ground so that it is ready to receive the seed.

We work on the mind and spirit of a person prior to their first step towards Christ. We put the nourishment into their spirits and uplift their minds so that they are ready to receive that first spiritual seed. Almost as though we get people ready before they take their first step towards Christ. Christian Radio assists with opening hearts and minds to be ready to receive Christ.

We work on putting good thoughts and little snippets of God into a person's life. These thoughts sit in their mind, working away, and they start thinking about all these things sub-consciously. A person may begin absolutely closed to the message of Christianity – a complete tough-nut, somebody who is anti-Christian, they don't want anything to do with it, they don't want to know about it, they swear black and blue that if they walk into a church the roof will cave in. That sort of person, through listening to Christian Radio, by themselves, in their car, **can become open to the gospel message**.

Christian Radio can and does reach into places that the local church can not go, however let me make one thing clear.

Your local Christian Radio station does not want to be anyone's church. What we are is the strategic media arm of the church, with the ability to get the message into places that the local church will never reach. **Think of your local Christian Radio station as being owned by your local church!**

Because media is such a powerful influencer, Christian Radio stations have sprung up all over the world. **Imagine what could be achieved when this mass media approach is in true partnership with the personal touch of hundreds of local churches undertaking evangelism and true discipleship!**

The strategy of Christian Radio is to *reach* people where they are now, to work on people *before* they walk into a church.

Strategies used by Christian Radio include...

- Broadcasting short thoughts on life and God throughout the day, to prepare the mind to be open to the gospel.
- Selecting songs whose lyrics uplift the spirits of people, to nourish the soul.
- Giving exposure to local pastors and churches to provide a link between the un-churched listener and the local church.
- Broadcasting personal testimonies which listeners can relate to.
- Being family friendly, - a 'clean' alternative to other radio stations.
- Some stations playing familiar mainstream music mixed in with Christian artists, to attract un-churched listeners.
- Encouraging and uplifting people to take the next step in their walk with God.
- Integration of radio and web-based media including social media.

Chapter 4

Real Stories: Lives Changed through Christian Radio

With the way radio works, you only ever get feedback from a handful of people, compared to how many are actually listening. Even though I get different stories on my desk every month, that's only a small portion of the lives that we're actually touching and changing through our ministry each and every day.

I'd like to share some stories of real lives changed, which listeners have told me during my work with Christian Radio. *Names have been changed.*

Here is *Sarah's* story...

> "I'd been sexually assaulted, my mother was murdered and recently my husband left me... I'd had the loss of a child... One night I was trying to tune my radio to a local rock station and I stumbled across the local Christian Radio station. I didn't realize it at the time, but as I listened to the music it just triggered something inside me. A song came on and it was a pretty emotional song and I hit the ground crying 'cause it was all about what my life was about and how to heal."

And today? **She's healing!**

She goes on to say...

> "I've been tuned in to the local Christian Radio ever since then, and it's been great.

It's changed my life! I started reading my Bible again and I went back to God."

Sarah also isn't keeping Christian Radio to herself.

"I recommend it to everyone!"

Christian Radio stations receive hundreds of these types of letters or emails throughout the year. And the interesting thing is that most follow a similar outline.

1. They had never heard of the local Christian Radio station,
2. They heard some songs they knew,
3. They then heard a Christian song or a 60 second *Positive Minute*, which are really thoughts on life and God,
4. They were really touched by what they heard, and could relate,
5. They have started reading their Bible again, or attending a church. They have found God through Christian Radio.

It's no coincidence that people randomly tune in to the local Christian Radio. Speaking from a spiritual point of view, I very much believe that it is God, the Holy Spirit, leading those people to hear something on the Christian Radio station at the right time, at the right place in their lives. Because of the strategic way Christian Radio is set up, God is able to reach people through it.

Here is *John's* story...

> "I was in a dark place in my life, so much so that I was driving my truck up one of the local mountains and was going to jump off the cliff... I was going to commit suicide. I was scanning through the radio because I wanted to hear one last song... and I came across the local Christian Radio station.
> A *Positive Minute* was playing from a Christian teacher, and it really touched me and made me reconsider what I was doing.

> I changed my mind about committing suicide and called a Christian friend, and asked him to come and help me, 'cos of what I was about to do."

If it wasn't for God convicting *John* through what he heard on Christian Radio at that exact moment, he wouldn't be with us today. He wouldn't have called his friend, he wouldn't have heard that positive thought, he wouldn't be alive.

And because of the strategic way that Christian Radio partners with local churches, we even see listeners getting regular solid discipleship as they find their home in a local church.

Here is *Ron's* story...

> "Just wanted to let you know how good and how much just listening to your station has helped and guided me. I had been through some real tough times.

My marriage had broken down, I was in trouble with the law and I was totally lost and without any hope. Through you guys [the local Christian Radio] I heard a church minister talking on your station and, thanks to God, found out he was the minister at a local church in my home town!"

Christian Radio connects people with the local church.

"I have started going to that church and have found God and Jesus and it has totally changed my life. **It has changed how I see the world and how I act.** I am only new with the Christian thing and am learning so much from the Bible and continually listening to you guys."

Remember how media influences culture? Remember that it changes how we view the world, how we think and act? I bet *Ron* had no concept of the subtle ways that media influences culture through hidden messages. But he still recognized that **what he heard on Christian Radio changed how he saw the world,** and changed how he acted!

And it's not just all about changing the lives of people who are in terrible situations either. Sometimes Christian Radio inspires people to act – encouraging them in their God given calling.

Here is *Leon's* story...

> "I just wanted to say thank you to everyone there at my local Christian Radio station, for helping me start on an adventure that God had planned for me to do. It was when I started listening to you that my life was finally heading in the right direction and

had my friend not told me about your station I don't know where I would be right now. So my deepest appreciation for this very special gift, I will always remember it."

Leon is now a missionary in South America. He is living out the call of God on his life, and he gives credit to the local Christian Radio station for setting him on the right path.

Christian Radio also works to inspire and encourage everyday Christians like you and me. It doesn't always have to be something dramatic or life changing – sometimes Christian Radio simply serves to encourage us in our daily lives.

Here is *Simon's* story...

"I started listening to Christian Radio in my car recently. It was time to make the switch after being challenged about the rubbish we put into our lives at Bible study one night - there is just too much rubbish on TV and on the other radio stations, and I knew listening to my Christian Radio station was one way I could cut a big part of that out of my life. I benefit daily from good Christian teaching which helps me to constantly be thinking about God's Word during the week, which has also helped to improve my spiritual health."

Christian Radio is a ministry which reaches people in the oddest of places, and helps people find direction in their life, and develop a deeper relationship with God.

Christian Radio Changes Lives by...

- Helping restore desperate people's lives.
- Reaching people at a critical moment with the right message.
- Directing people to a local church family.
- Challenging people to commit to the call of God on their lives.
- Encouraging people to stay positive throughout their day.

PART TWO
Using Christian Radio

POWERFUL CHRISTIAN RADIO

Chapter 5

The 21st Century Church

In this chapter I'd like to discuss an issue which I feel is very important, not just in partnering with Christian Radio, but in understanding Christianity in relation to the society we live in.

We live in the 21st Century, and yet we present a 20th Century church. Certainly the style of many church services is the same as it was hundreds of years ago, and this is one part of the problem. But what I am mainly concerned about is that **the thinking and strategy of the modern church has not changed**, and has become unsuitable for use in a 21st Century society.

In the mid 20th Century the church could count on most people attending each Sunday and generally seeing themselves as 'good Christians'. Even in the later 20th Century the church could still rightly assume that most people had some exposure to Sunday School and would have a basic understanding of the Christian story. Even when I was younger I remember we *had* to say the Lord's Prayer each morning – and this was at a public primary school!

This is no longer the case. In the 21st Century we live in an increasingly pluralistic society full of many beliefs. Today most people aged 40 and under have never been to church because their parents never took them. **So our society is now filled with a generation who has no idea of the basics of Christianity.** They see the church as irrelevant and ridiculous. In the 21st Century **we do not live in a Christian culture** and it's important that the church recognizes that, and examines methods to address this issue.

We *must* stop using any Christian jargon and images because the society we live in has no clue what they mean. As my pastor often says about evangelizing people in our city, **we may as well be living in Borneo** – because the level of awareness of the Christian message is the same. **Our society has changed, but the way we do church, missions and outreach remains the same.** We need to find new ways to evangelize as essentially **we now live in a pagan society,** which has no understanding of the Christian faith.

In the book *Unique: Telling your story in the age of brands and social media,* by Phil Cooke, he provides an interesting example of just how 'not-at-all-Christian' our society is today.

> I drove down secretly one morning to look for a Christmas gift for my wife, Kathleen. As I was shopping, I began watching a young couple looking for a necklace. The dealer brought out a beautiful tray of cross necklaces ranging from simple, contemporary designs to more traditional designs featuring Jesus hanging on the cross.

> The young couple was very impressed, and as they looked down the row of crosses, the woman became interested in the Catholic-looking style design with the figure of Jesus on the cross.
>
> She looked puzzled and said to the salesman, "I don't understand. Who's that little guy hanging on that cross necklace?"
>
> She was at least 25 years old, but she had absolutely no idea who that 'little guy' was or what He was doing on that necklace.

This is a great example of how unaware most people are about the basic story of Christianity. I have previously noted in this book that **most listeners to Christian Radio do not attend church**, even though they refer to themselves as 'Christian'. To me this indicates that today people say they are Christian, without any real understanding of what that actually means. They say 'Christian' and mean 'nice person who tries to live a good life.'

Here's another example. A friend of mine is a church pastor in a small beach town on the south-east coast of Australia. When he first arrived at his church he wanted to do a big dramatic Easter parade, depicting the Easter story, through the main street of the town. He thought this would be a good way to engage with the local community.

On chatting to another church pastor about the idea he discovered that a similar street theater performance of the *Stations of the Cross* was performed last year. However the feedback they received from the general community was that no one knew what the performance was about. **They had no idea it was even Jesus up on the cross!** They had no idea of the basic Christian *story*.

In the 20th Century the church would count on people going to them to hear the message. But in the 21st Century **people expect information to come to them**. And the information comes swiftly and rapidly to them through Facebook, Twitter, Email, TV, Radio, iTunes, On-demand movies, and whatever the next social media invention is.

This is why most radio stations not only broadcast on AM or FM but they also stream online (Internet radio). In fact, some Christian Radio stations have multiple streams, covering a variety of tastes and styles.

We need to change our thinking. Stop expecting people to come to us. We need to do what Jesus did, not expecting people to come to him and hear him in the temple, but to sit by the woman at the well. To go to where the people are – going into the tax-collector's home. **That's what Jesus did... and that's exactly what radio does today!** Radio is with people all day long, and then we go home with them too.

Today most people don't know, or don't remember the *story* of Christianity. **They don't remember what God did for humanity.** People haven't stopped attending church because it's boring... they aren't attending because they don't know the *story*. And because they aren't turning up to church they now have a misguided idea of God, the church and Christianity.

I mentioned before that media is our biggest cultural influencer today – and it influences by telling *stories*. For the most part, people today get their impression and understanding of God and Christianity exclusively through media. **So it is essential that the church of the 21st Century understands how to influence culture through media.** The church needs to take a page from Jesus' book and start telling stories again. Stories told through entertainment, which our society can relate to and understand the message.

There has never been a better time for the local church and individual Christians to learn how to use modern media effectively – including using the local Christian Radio station.

The 21st Century Church needs to Understand...

- We do not live in a Christian culture.
- Most people do not know the basic story of Christianity.
- People do not understand our jargon or symbols – some don't even recognize the 'guy on the cross' is Jesus!
- We must go to where the people are, as they have stopped coming to us.
- Media – we need to use media effectively.

POWERFUL CHRISTIAN RADIO

Chapter 6

Christian Radio in Friendship Evangelism

Christian Radio belongs in the realm of pre-evangelism or friendship evangelism. It may sound funny but this is the evangelism that happens before evangelism. It's all about developing a relationship with somebody, before you even mention Jesus, God or church.

You've probably been encouraged by your pastor *many times* to invite your friends and family along to a church event – particularly if it's an outreach event. Or maybe your pastor just wants you to bring your family along on a Sunday morning. I mean isn't this a fair enough request?

Well I don't know if you've noticed, but **it's really hard to get your family and friends along to your church**. You feel uncomfortable and awkward every time you ask, because you know the answer is always no. And if they won't even come to church with you, how on earth are you ever going to have a conversation about God with them?

The reality is we don't live in a Christian society and just like most people, your family and friends have a warped idea of what the church is all about. They are not comfortable with stepping foot inside a church or even going to some outreach event. They are simply not ready to step in through the doors of a church.

This is where your local Christian Radio station comes into play. They present a family friendly entertainment option, and are often the first port of call for someone wanting to clean up their life. Christian Radio is one of the easiest places to point your family and friends to. Because of its structure and format **people will tune in to radio, before they are ready to go to church with you**.

By simply making your family and friends *aware* of the local Christian Radio station, you are laying a foundation which can be built upon later. Mentioning some of the things you love about the station, or finding a point of interest for the person you are speaking to, is a great way to connect them with Christian Radio.

Okay, but what do I actually say?

Scenario 1: You have invited your friend to church so many times and you have just asked once again – they say no, again.

> "That's okay, I understand that you're not ready to go to church, but look, you may want to check out the local Christian Radio station because I know you've got kids and they're the only local

> radio station that is actually safe for little ears."

Scenario 2: You are over 75 years old and don't listen to the local Christian Radio because you don't like pop music. You are chatting to your daughter who has post-natal depression.

> "Look I'm a bit old for the music they play, but I still support the station because I know of all the people they encourage throughout the day. Maybe if you tuned in, it would help you feel better while you are stuck at home."

Scenario 3: A friend comments that they never play a certain singer on radio any more. You know that the Christian Radio station does still play that artist.

> "Yeah, but XYZ Station still plays him. If you want to hear him on radio just tune into them!"

You see at this stage, you don't even have to mention that the station you are pointing them to is 'Christian'. That just doesn't need to come up yet in the conversation.

Scenario 4: Your neighbor is explaining that he has no problem with Jesus, but hates the church.

> "Well did you know there's a Christian Radio station locally?"

They can learn more about Jesus by listening to Christian Radio, before they are ready to attend church.

Scenario 5: A work mate comments how sick they are of all the rubbish and dirty jokes on the radio.

> "Oh? Have you heard of XYZ FM? They are totally family focused and don't have any rude jokes or inappropriate comments."

Scenario 6: Your brother says that he's had a terrible year and he can't wait for this year to be over. He says he's just discouraged all the time.

> "Well, I listen to XYZ FM all day and they play these *Positive Minutes* in between songs, and they really lift me up and make me feel good. They remind me that life is worth living."

Most of the people you speak to will have never heard of the local Christian Radio station. So, sure it benefits the station when you tell people about it. But the purpose in getting them to listen is to start them on a journey towards Christ, even though at the moment they are closed to the concept. **Make them aware that there is a positive alternative**, and see where God moves them next.

Christian Radio belongs to the local church. Primarily working in pre-evangelism, lifting people up, encouraging them throughout their day. Giving them a little taste – a hint of God.

Use Christian Radio to bring your Family & Friends to Christ by...

- Making them aware of the local Christian Radio.
- Looking for needs they have which the Christian Radio station can fill.
- Suggesting they should listen to the Christian Radio if they are not ready to attend church.

POWERFUL CHRISTIAN RADIO

Chapter 7

11 Ways the Church can Partner with Christian Radio

A local Christian Radio station should acknowledge that it *belongs* to the local church. This would not normally be any kind of legal ownership, but in a moral or spiritual sense. (That is, we are here to *serve* the local church.) Christian Radio stations usually have a very large amount of listeners who are open to the Christian message – **but do not attend church**. In my experience I have seen stations with over 80% of their listeners in this category.

This presents an obvious opportunity to link Christian Radio and the local church together, bringing those who embrace Christian values into the local church for teaching, which may bring them to faith, and grow them into a mature walk. **If the local church wants to reach the *low hanging fruit* (people already open to the gospel) they can target listeners to Christian Radio.**

Christian Radio is not trying to be a church – **but we *are* designed to be a powerful resource to the church**. The *media arm* of the local church.

This chapter presents 11 practical examples of ways a local church may be able to partner with the local Christian Radio. These examples may require some changes and understanding from both parties, however the following list are from real life scenarios. They are 11 straightforward ways to bring the local church and Christian Radio together.

**Disclaimer: The following are examples. Your local Christian Radio station may or may not be able to do all of these examples due to their individual circumstances.

Number 1: Easter & Christmas Messages.

Possibly the simplest way for the local church and Christian Radio to connect is by airing short pre-recorded greetings from local church pastors at Easter and Christmas. These would each be between 60 seconds to 2 minutes long and would be part mini-sermon and part plug for your seasonal church services.

> "Hi this is pastor Josh Reid from St. Joseph Campbell's Church. As you sit down with your family this Christmas I would like to encourage you to consider the true meaning for the season. Most of us have a vague idea that we are celebrating the birth of Jesus Christ. That He came into our world as a baby and grew up to become a man who would die on the cross (which we celebrate at Easter). And we know that during His life Jesus healed

people from sickness, walked on water, and gave us the story of the good Samaritan (whatever a Samaritan is). But do we *really* understand that at Christmas we celebrate the gift of a new beginning and a second chance – for you and me and all of humanity? Because you see, you can not have the story of Christmas, without the story of Easter. They are two parts of the one story. So as you give your gifts this Christmas day, take a moment to remember the One who gave you the best gift ever. You can join us at St. Joseph Campbell's Church on Christmas morning at 7am and 10am on the corner of Market Street and Moyers Avenue in the city."

Now, I'm sure you could come up with something better than that. So what's stopping you?

Call up your local Christian Radio and offer to record such a greeting. You are providing good, timely content for your local station, and this provides both parties with **a timely opportunity to reach all those un-churched listeners within your community**. And let's face it, Easter and Christmas are the two best chances we have each year to actually get people into a church building!

If you are a Christian Radio station you might like to be proactive and email all the pastors in your area inviting them to record such a message.

Number 2: Positive Minutes.

Many Christian Radio stations are in the habit of playing 60 second audio spots by a variety of Christian teachers, throughout the day. These are generally either called *God Spots* or *Positive Minutes*. The spots are thoughts on life and God. Some are more like mini-sermons, while others are little stories that encourage and uplift people who tune in. The structure in creating these spots is simple; *one thought for one minute.* So keep it simple, and don't cramp more than one thought into each 60 second spot.

When I started in Christian Radio all of these spots were by Christian pastors or teachers who were well known around the country. But after a while we approached several local pastors and Christian leaders to create their own spots locally. **This worked really well, resulting in a closer connection with our listeners.** A few of these spots we produced locally, ended up being picked up by other Christian Radio stations and are now being broadcast nationally. Essentially expanding the profile of our local pastors across the nation.

Here's an example of a spot produced by a local pastor from Wollongong, Australia:

> "I watched with great interest recently the rescue of a French sailor, by an Australian cruise ship. It was cruising the beautiful waters of Tasmania. Once the mayday call was received the captain didn't wait for someone else to respond. But he changed course. Not for 4 hours, not for 10 hours, not even for 24 hours – but

for a staggering 53 hours, away from the direction they were originally heading! In essence the cruise ship became a rescue boat. Isn't that a picture of the type of church we are meant to lead or even attend? I love what Jesus does in Matthew 18:11. He tells the parable of the shepherd who left the 99 to go after the one. I have a question for you today as a leader of a business, at work or even a church – are you captaining a cruise ship or a rescue boat? Sometimes we get so busy meeting the needs of the many that we forget which it is. You know, it will never be convenient to lead your people toward rescuing stranded people, but it's what Jesus asked us to do. I'm Paul Bartlett from adifferentlight.org."

Producing local *Positive Minutes* gives local pastors and their church more exposure in the community. **As a pastor of a local church, being on-air may bring people into your church on a Sunday morning.** Some pastors have facilities to record spots at their own church, while others come into the radio station. The only commitment the radio station would need from the pastor, is to keep a fresh flow of new spots coming in each month. You may have to write and record another 15 per month, for example.

While a radio station couldn't possibly get *every* pastor in their area to produce spots (as they would not have enough air space) this may be something to consider for yourself and your church.

Number 3: Weekly Interview Show for Local Pastors.

For several years, *Pulse 94.1* in Wollongong, Australia produced a local weekly program called *Straight To The Heart*, where a local pastor is interviewed about their ministry journey. This is a very personal interview, which is pre-recorded and then cut into 5 minute segments. Once it goes to air the 5 or 6 five minute segments are played over an hour with music and ads in between.

The result of this program has been that listeners have heard a pastor on-air and then actually **turned up to that pastor's church the following Sunday morning!** A direct result from hearing a radio interview of a local church pastor.

Straight To The Heart is a simple concept. There is a host, who in this example is also a local pastor, and they record at least one interview each week. Sometimes they pre-record up to three each Friday, so that after a month or so the station is 4 to 6 months ahead. Then they air the show on a Friday morning and repeat it Sunday nights.

There are around 200 churches in the Wollongong area, so they make sure they interview pastors from a wide variety of denominations so that no-one feels left out. **They created this show so that church pastors could get on radio and talk about their own journey into Christianity and their calling to become a pastor.**

This show is one very practical way where the local church can partner and link in with the local Christian Radio station. **It is an easy template for other Christian Radio stations to copy** and produce their own similar show for their own local church pastors. Linking the local church and the greater community, through radio.

Number 4: Free Church Announcements.

Your local Christian Radio station may provide free Community Service Announcements (CSAs) to the general public. These are usually read out live by on-air announcers. Other times they are pre-recorded with a bit more production to make them sound better. Sometimes the announcer may read out the full details of the event, but this can get long-winded and boring for the listener. These days the announcer will usually rattle off a few CSAs at once and then refer listeners to the station's website for further details. But no matter how your particular local Christian Radio station prefers to do them, the important point is that they probably do provide such a service.

There is often some criteria to get your church's event on the CSA roster. Normally it must be a not-for-profit event and/or literally a *service to the community*. And usually the event would be free to attend. Therefore the station **can include** church fetes, family fun days, men's breakfasts, a special guest speaker at your church, ladies lunches, craft days, kids clubs, free car-wash, and various outreach events. A *church conference* would **not** fit into a CSA (but keep reading to find out how they *can* get your conference on air).

Getting your event announced as a CSA is a straight forward process. Normally you can phone or fax it in, email it, or fill in the form of the radio's website. Check the procedure with your own local Christian Radio station.

HOWEVER – your Christian Radio station is not sitting around all day waiting for your call. **They are busy**, usually punching well above their weight and steering a very tight ship. So do yourself a favor and plan ahead. Don't call up on Friday afternoon with an event you have this Sunday! (You would be surprised how often this has happened to me.) It will not have time to get on-air!

So plan ahead and give the radio station at least 3 weeks notice leading up to your event. Best practice is as soon as you know about the event – **contact your Christian Radio station immediately**. If you call on too short notice they won't be able to help you.

I'd encourage you to take advantage of this great free service - but please give your Christian Radio station plenty of notice!

Number 5: Co-Sponsorship of Your Event.

Some church events do not fit into the free CSA category. A church conference would be the prime example. However there are other ways to promote your church event on your Christian Radio station. One way is through a *Co-Sponsorship agreement* with your Christian Radio station.

Co-Sponsorship could include events that have a fee attached such as a church conference, or a band performance, but could also apply to a much larger free event, such as a Community Christmas Carols.

How this would work is that your Christian Radio station becomes the official *Media Partner* and therefore a major sponsor of your event. This means you would be required to place their logo on all your posters, brochures, website and other marketing materials. Plus have space for a promotional booth for the radio station, at your event. You would also allow the station to put up banners or flags at the event, in a prime location.

In exchange your Christian Radio station may provide production of your advert, or air-time promoting your event, for free. With a four week lead up to the event, the on-air component would be worth tens of thousands of dollars in advertising revenue! (This is why the station would become a major sponsor of your event.)

In summary, the church puts the Christian Radio station's logo everywhere, and they give you HEAPS of radio advertising space!

However, as per my caution in *Number 4*, a Co-Sponsorship can not be organized at short notice. How much notice needed would depend on the event, but I would suggest a minimum of 3 months notice. Consider that just like your church does, the Christian Radio station also plans their calendar at least 12 months ahead. **So if you already know you have a conference** or a famous band or international speaker, or a massive Christmas or Easter event coming up – **now is the time to speak to the Christian Radio** about a *Co-Sponsorship agreement*.

If available sometimes a *Co-Sponsorship agreement* with your Christian Radio station may include their announcers MC-ing the event for you, or even **broadcasting live** from the event. (see *Number 7*.)

Number 6: Radio Advertising.

If a *Co-Sponsorship* arrangement isn't right for your event or church, then you can also look at *Paid Radio Advertising* on your local Christian Radio. This is also a great way to financially support your local station, if you have the means.

Your local Christian Radio station may have very competitive rates compared to other radio stations, but they also may have a standard discount for churches and Christian organizations. So it would be wise to at least inquire what their standard rates are, and if they have a church discount.

A Christian Radio station operates differently to a commercial station, mainly because it has a different purpose. For example in Australia, most of the Christian Radio stations are on *Community Radio licenses*, which means they are **limited to only 5 minutes per hour for radio advertising**. (In fact it is technically not *advertising* but *Station Sponsorship* – I use the term advertising in this book simply as a common term.)

I would also encourage any church to not only look at the published rates sheet, but to have a conversation with your Christian Radio station to see if a compromise could be found to fit into your budget. It doesn't hurt to ask.

If you do happen to have missed the cut off point for Co-Sponsorship, radio advertising can be a very viable option for your church, as ads can be arranged and put on air at very short notice.

A final note on radio advertising. You are normally looking at a 30 second spot. This should include the information about your event, including the date. And it should *point to* somewhere that the listener can get further information or sign up. Good places to point to are a website, a physical address or land-line phone number. Bad places to point to are an email, a cell phone number, or any number that is too long. **Your ad will be more effective if the place you are pointing to is easy to remember.**

Number 7: Live Outside Broadcast.

Your Christian Radio station may be able to conduct a live *Outside Broadcast* at your event (an OB).

Often this is in addition to a Co-Sponsorship agreement. So rather than just having a promotional booth, the station would actually also broadcast live - essentially setting up a makeshift studio at your event.

There are various technical requirements needed in order to conduct an OB, and you would need to talk specifics with your Christian Radio station. The possibility of an OB may also depend on the location of your event – for example if there is no phone or mobile data signal where your event is, an OB would be close to impossible.

There are two types of OB. The first is where the station crew would set up a studio on-site at your event and broadcast from there. They would play their normal line-up of music and ads, but in the talk breaks they would be speaking all about the great things happening at your event. The announcers would encourage listeners who are driving around in their cars to stop by and experience the event. Having a live radio station at your event also creates a bit of hype for the people there.

The second type is basically a simulcast of your event. So whatever you say from the stage is broadcast across the radio frequency in real time. This could be appropriate for a Christmas Carols, a band performance, a political debate, or anything that is big enough and of interest enough to the wider community. I should also note that a simulcast requires much more technical equipment and expertise. It is difficult to do right and a lot of hard work. But it *may* be possible.

Number 8: News service.

Depending on the size of your local Christian Radio they may provide a local news service. Some stations who can not afford to hire journalists, develop a relationship with their local University or journalism school and use students as volunteer journalists. If such a service is available in your area, it would be a great idea to contact the station with anything that you feel is newsworthy. As a church this may include, a new building opening, a new pastor appointed at your church, or something special your church has done, or is about to do, in your community.

You can simply submit a media release to the station, or if you are unsure about that, call the station to discuss your project or news item. This is a nice simple way to use radio to let people other than your congregation know what you are doing.

Number 9: Sunday Night Sermons.

Many Christian Radio stations play a show called *Sunday Night Sermons* (or something similarly named). This is a very simple, low production effort which grabs pre-recorded sermons from local pastors and airs them on radio.

Most churches today record all their Sunday sermons. Usually these are already in digital format, rather than on a *cassette player*. (Remember them?) So all the church needs to do is deliver the sermons to your Christian Radio station (via CD, email, drop-box etc.) with a summary of what is in each sermon, who it's by, and the time length of it. Because some smaller stations will not have time to listen to the whole recording, they may rely on the church to be accurate about what is on the audio track.

Most churches already place their sermons on their own website. This is nice, but the reality is that most of the people who go to your website, already attend your church. **With getting your sermons on radio you are reaching a multitude of people, most who do not attend any church.**

Number 10: Volunteer Show Host.

Maybe you are a pastor with a passion for broadcasting? Maybe not. Maybe you have someone in your church who is though. Providing a volunteer host for a show or shift on your local Christian Radio is a great way to develop a solid ongoing relationship with the station.

In my work with Christian Radio I have seen pastors host shows such as *Straight To The Heart* as well as hosting the Sunday morning praise & worship hour. Particularly at stations which are not in capital city areas, the use of volunteers is essential. So even if hosting a radio show is not for you, encourage your congregation to volunteer. *This example may not be available at bigger stations who already have announcers on staff.*

Number 11: Produce Your Own Show!

This final example of a way the local church may partner with the Christian Radio station is a bigger one. In fact it would probably not be feasible for a single church to do. It would only be possible if a group of similar minded churches, or a whole denomination in an area **worked together**. And once again it would depend on your station's particular situation too.

Having said that, it is not out of the question for a church group to produce their own weekly show for the local Christian Radio station. In fact this has happened at *Pulse 94.1* in Wollongong, Australia.

They formed a partnership with the Catholic Diocese of Wollongong. So this was not just one church, but all the Catholic Churches and Catholic Schools across four regions. Plus the arrangement was between the radio station and the local Bishop's office.

The partnership arrangement was that the church would produce and provide *a weekly show* targeting local Catholic listeners. The show would be very ecumenical and wouldn't have anything controversial or 'too Catholic' in it.

In exchange the Catholic Bishop's office would heavily promote the local Christian Radio station throughout *all* their churches and *all* their schools across four regions. The first stage was by hanging a poster about the show in each church, and handing out brochures in all the schools. There were also various articles about the new show on the Christian Radio station, in Catholic magazines.

The result of this was that almost overnight thousands and thousands of church attending Catholics, plus all the school students and their families, were suddenly made aware of the Christian Radio station, and were being encouraged by the Bishop to tune in.

This benefited both parties. The Catholics got their own show, which they used as a way of reaching out to non-church attending Catholic Christians. And the Christian Radio increased their weekly listeners by thousands, because of the proactive way the church promoted the show.

This show, *The Journey*, didn't require any ongoing work from the Christian Radio station, as the Catholic Church produced it off-site. They then forwarded the show to the station, and it was simply programmed in.

So yes, *Number 11* is quite a big project, but there's no reason that a church or group of churches couldn't create a similar show for their own Christian Radio station. It may help the station, and at the same time promotes the church. Now you might be thinking that there is no way that your church would have resources enough to do this – but **there's no reason that you can't meet with a representative from your Christian Radio station and have a conversation,** about how you could partner with them.

We *need* to work together to fulfill God's vision for our community. Christian Radio and the local church working together in Kingdom growth. The Christian media *serving* the church. But equally as important, the local church *understanding* the ministry of Christian Radio. A key result will be churches growing in spiritual depth, becoming more relevant, and resulting in growth in numbers.

This list of 11 examples is by no means complete, **and some may not be possible at your local station**. There are many other great examples out there. The reason I have chosen these 11 is that most are simple examples that even the smallest of stations and churches can pull together.

You might work for a Christian Radio who is not doing anything to link in with the local church. Or you might be a pastor of a local church that is not taking advantage of the local Christian Radio station. Get on the phone. **It's time to start the conversation!**

11 Ways Your Church can Partner with Christian Radio...

- Provide an Easter or Christmas message.
- Record a series of *Positive Minutes*.
- Be interviewed on a program for pastors.
- Promote your church event for free.
- Get your Christian Radio to sponsor your event.
- Advertise your event on radio.
- Get the station to broadcast live from your event.
- Submit a *media release* to their news service.
- Get your sermon played on radio.
- Host a show (or find someone in your church).
- Produce your own show.

Chapter 8

Importance of Supporting Christian Radio

Late one night, my phone rang with a number I didn't recognize... I was at home, stressed about how on earth I was going to raise an amount of $44,407 for the upcoming Christian Radio appeal at the station I worked at. This was a *very* large amount of money for us at the time and it seemed almost impossible that we would reach it, as previous appeals had only brought in half that amount.

"The phone call can wait", I thought as I ignored it and let it ring out. "It's probably a telemarketer anyway. And besides who calls at this hour!?"

But before I sat down I felt an inner 'nudge' and decided to return the missed call. I had no idea who it would be.

The call was from an old friend of mine who I hadn't seen or heard from in years. In fact he now lived on the opposite side of the country. We caught up quickly and shared a joke. Then a pause as I was still waiting to hear what he was calling about.

He said that he had received my letter from the Christian Radio station about the upcoming appeal and the things we needed to raise money for.

Although he no longer lived in the area he had given our office his new address as he wanted to stay in touch with us. And right then a wave of discouragement dumped on me. I suddenly wished that I hadn't returned the call, because I was *just so sure* that he was about to complain about receiving the letter, or perhaps how he didn't believe in fund-raising and was calling to tell me off. I admit I am not always a positive thinker! But (oh *me* of little faith) he said nothing of the sort.

My friend said that he had always wanted to support our Christian Radio station and felt that he was currently in a position to make a *substantial contribution*. Well now I was listening! He said that he *understood* Christian Radio, loved our sound and understood the needs we were raising funds for.

He then commented that the large organization which he worked for, will match any donation that an employee makes with an equal amount. Essentially doubling the donation he was about to make. This was good news indeed, and in fact I was familiar with his employer's matching program. My friend then said that right now the organization is matching all donations by 2 for 1. To be clear his employer would give two dollars for every dollar he gave to us.

My night was starting to look up.

Eventually he gave me his credit card details and then I asked the golden question, how much would he like to donate?

"Seven grand." he said.

"Uhhhhhh..." I said.

"That means $7000." he said.

"Uhh, yeah – sure I know what 'grand' means, but well, it's just that we've never received a donation that large before." I replied.

And then he reminded me that his employer will now match it 2 for 1. That is – they will donate another $14,000 on top of his $7000. A total donation of $21,000.

We chatted for a little longer, I thanked him for his donation – several times, and finally got off the phone. After I hung up I thought how glad I was that I responded to the 'nudge' and returned the call. The end result being that a $21,000 donation from *an unexpected place* that night, now made my goal of $44,407 much more achievable.

A few days later I contacted him again to thank him for his donation. I commented that we were so overwhelmed by his donation that - through him - God provided from such an unexpected place. I asked if I could use his story to encourage others to also give from an *unexpected place*?

While he was happy that I was excited, **he saw his giving from a different perspective**. He said that from our point of view God blessed the radio station from an unexpected place – and that was right, **but the reason he gave came from a different motivation**.

The story on his end is actually about God's blessing overflowing into generosity. He commented that they - he and his wife - have recently been blessed in abundance and this donation was only a small portion of that blessing overflowing into something that they believe has the heart of God. (The local Christian Radio station.) He was happy for me to use his story to challenge listeners, but he would challenge them from a different motivation.

He wanted to challenge listeners, that they would acknowledge areas where God has been good, be thankful to Him and let that thankfulness overflow into generosity – to Christian Radio, sure, but also in life.

This story about my friend's blessing highlights an important issue. **That in most cases Christian Radio relies heavily on financial donations from listeners and supporters**. That is the primary revenue source for Christian Radio, and without listeners donating, Christian Radio would cease to exist.

Christian Radio stations are modern day missionaries. Going out into places that the local church can never reach by themselves. Using modern media disguised as entertainment, they proclaim the gospel message directly to where the people are. They are a powerful, far reaching ministry that *prepares* people to receive the Christian message, long before they are ready to attend church.

So I would encourage you to consider the message in this book, and to view Christian Radio for what it is – **a ministry that evangelizes through media**. And to understand that, just like traditional missionaries, Christian Radio *does* need your prayers and financial support.

I pray, just like my friend did, that *you* would acknowledge areas where God has been good, be thankful to Him and let that thankfulness overflow into generosity – sure to Christian Radio, but also in your whole life.

God bless you.
Josh Reid

Credits

- McKee, Robert. Story: Substance, Structure, Style, and the Principles of Screenwriting. London: Methuen Publishing Limited, 1998.
- Johnston, Robert K. Useless Beauty: Ecclesiastes Through the Lens of Contemporary Film. Grand Rapids: Baker Academic, 2004 . *As cited in* Cooke, Phil. Jolt: Get The Jump On a World That's Constantly Changing. Nashville: Thomas Nelson, 2011.
- Cooke, Phil. Unique: Telling Your Story in the Age of Brands and Social Media. California: Regal Books, 2012.
- Bartlett, Paul. www.adifferentlight.org.
- Newell, Mike. Four Weddings and a Funeral. PolyGram Filmed Entertainment, 1994. http://www.imdb.com/title/tt0109831/?ref_=nv_sr_1

For their editorial input, feedback and comments as I drafted this book:

Berni Dymet, David Smith, Alan Rich, Phil Edwards, Loretta Reid, Mark Jeffery, Ray Robinson, Michael Kohler, Bruce McLennan, Geoff Moses, Nada Appleby, Phil Cooke, Jonar Nader, Gavin Brett, Kim Wilkinson, Stephen Wilkinson, Marilyn Munoz-Vogt, Jodie McGill, Darren Robinson, Jeff Foster, Graeme Burrill, Frank Dickinson, Mark Reddy, Rick Dunham, Nathan Brown, Joshua Crowther, Nikki Hart, Martin Bragger, Peter Pilt, Darryl Stewart, Werner Egger, Brett McLeod, Peter Chapman, Arnie Cole, Karl Faase, Clayton Childs, Peter Irvine.

Acknowledgments

I did not intend to write this book. In fact I was very surprised to discover that such a book did not already exist. But even after extensive research I could not find a book, let alone a blog article, specifically on how the *ministry* of Christian Radio works. There were a few books on the history of Christian Radio, but none explaining how the ministry of (how God works through) Christian Radio takes place. Which is ironic because the frustration of many Christian Radio professionals is that people simply don't get what it is that we do. We have trouble explaining exactly why we are a ministry and how on earth that actually fits into 'God's Kingdom'.

So even though I had little interest in becoming 'an author', about Christian Radio, various circumstances have led me to write this little book, which explains in practical terms, the strategy, impact and ministry of a local Christian Radio station.

There are many people who have contributed to this book, either through frustrating me beyond belief, or through constant support and encouragement over many years, as I began to put my thoughts on the topic, into words that actually made sense. It would be inappropriate to mention those who frustrated me with their closed views on Christian Radio, but I would like to highlight a few special people who have provided me the encouragement and support needed in completing this book.

My mentor, Alan Rich, who guided my thoughts and mental attitude, completely changing the way I now think and view life.

My dedicated team at Pulse 94.1: Darren Robinson, Graeme Burrill, Jeff Foster, Jodie McGill and Marilyn Munoz-Vogt, who all keep the wheels turning and ensure I stay focused on the end goal.

My board at Pulse 94.1: Mark Jeffery, Michael Kohler, Bruce McLennan and Ray Robinson, who allow me to be creative in my role, freeing me to do the many speaking engagements and other projects, like writing this book.

To Phil Cooke, who challenged and inspired me for years before we even met. His books and daily blog have been essential to the development of my thinking, and my understanding of the best ways for Christians to engage modern culture through media.

To Jonar Nader, who taught me the many benefits of thinking way outside of the box.

Finally to my wife Loretta and my children, Jackson, Dylan and our little girl, Mackenzie, who continually put up with my mood swings, my early mornings and my late nights, as I run around trying to make films and write books in my spare time. Thank you for your patience!

And to all those people who have frustrated me as I tried to explain the purpose of Christian Radio stations – thank you! You provided all the material for this book.

Thanks for reading.

Josh Reid
26th February, 2014

About the Author

Josh Reid, an Australian media professional involved in producing film, television and radio, writes and speaks internationally on the influence media has on our culture. Through his speaking engagements and online blog at joshreidmedia.com, he challenges us to use media effectively in engaging with our 21st Century society. CEO of Earl Street Pictures, the feature film production company behind *1500 Steps*, he is a 20 year veteran of stage and screen, having worked in over 9 countries, mainly in the third world. As General Manager of Christian Radio Pulse 94.1, Josh strategically took a struggling regional station and grew it into a thriving, sustainable, powerful media resource, focusing on direct links between the local church and un-churched radio listeners. Josh is available to speak at your conference or church event, and will entertain and challenge your audience to think about media differently. Reid lives in Wollongong, Australia, with his wife Loretta, two sons, Jackson and Dylan, and daughter Mackenzie.

Find out more at JoshReidMedia.com
Follow on Twitter @joshreidmedia
Facebook.com/JoshReidMedia
Email: josh@joshreidmedia.com

Josh Reid is available to speak at your church, conference or radio station event.

Bulk copies of this book can be ordered for your radio station or organization. The cover can be customized with your station's logo on the outside, and back pages, like this one, can be customized with your station's information.

For booking Josh Reid or for customized book orders please go to JoshReidMedia.com or email: josh@joshreidmedia.com

POWERFUL CHRISTIAN RADIO

JoshReidMedia.com

www.ingramcontent.com/pod-product-compliance
Lightning Source LLC
Chambersburg PA
CBHW071721040426
42446CB00011B/2164